Mila's Star of the Week Story

PDCD is an inborn error of metabolism that prevents people from using their food for cellular energy. People with **PDCD** suffer from poor muscle tone, neurological damage, developmental delays, lethargy, and organ damage. The prognosis for children with **PDCD** is a life expectancy of about 3 years; prognosis is based on multiple variables.

To learn more about **PDCD** or help, please contact Mother of PDCD Warrior/Nurse/Non-Profit Organizer, Emma Watt **http://www.pdcdresearchfund.com**

Motivational credits to Cousin-Writer-Photographer, Mick Schulte and Friend-Writer, Barb Danson.

To order additional copies of this book, contact:
Xlibris
844-714-8691
www.Xlibris.com
Orders@Xlibris.com

ISBN: 978-1-6698-3728-2 (sc)
ISBN: 978-1-6698-3729-9 (e)

Print information available on the last page

Rev. date: 08/22/2022

Hi, my name is Mila, Princess
Warrior to my family & friends.
I conquer battles through
every day's end.

The battles I fight aren't
amazing to you
because you're healthy, normal
things are easy to do.

Like you, I can hear, feel,
talk, eat and see.
But I was born with a
disease called, PDCD.

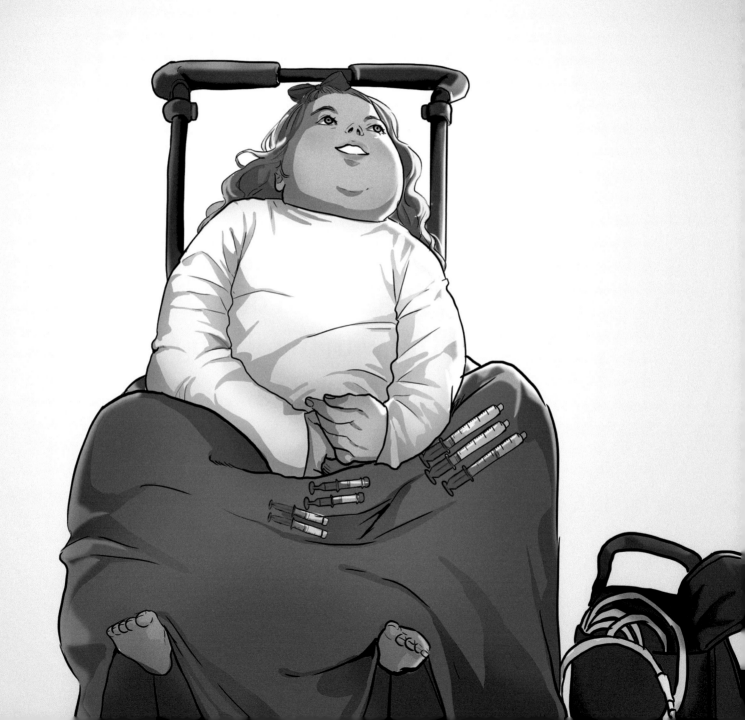

I have three sisters, a
Mom, Dad and a dog.
They battle with me through
frightening fog.

I'm tired a lot so I'm a
really good sleeper.
My sister says I'm the
best secret keeper.

My muscles are weak so I
need help just to sit.
A noisy suction helps so I
don't choke on my spit.

I don't eat by mouth, but
through a tube in my tummy.
My food smells like cake
mix, so very yummy.

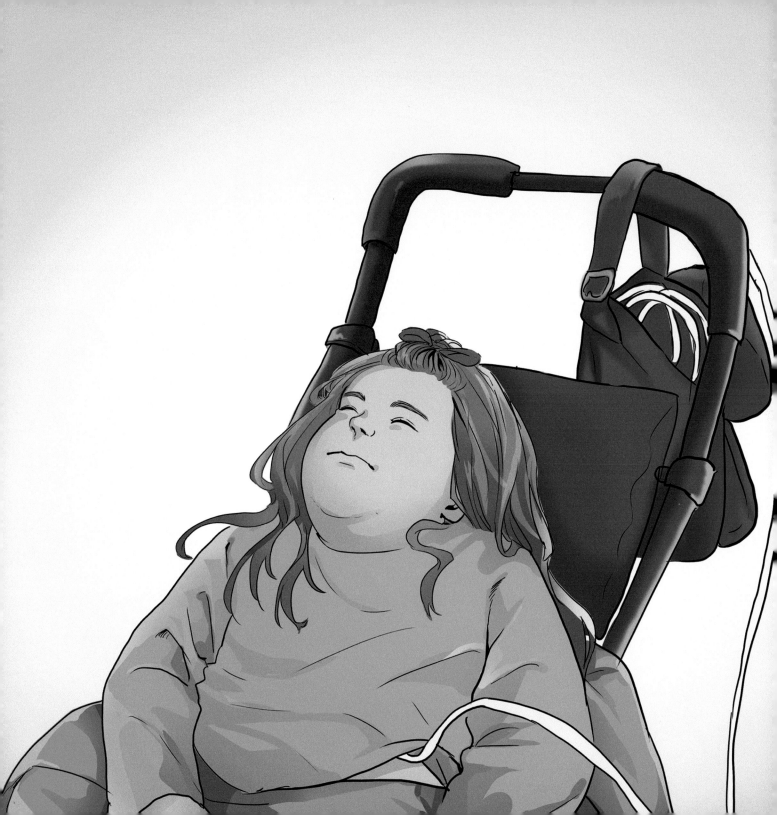

I need a nurse to bring me to school.
And don't understand quiet time rules.

I'm non-verbal, which means
I can't say my words.
I moan when I'm sad and ramble
to sing with the birds.

School is fun. I love to be here with you!
It's hard for me to learn but
you help me through.

I hear you talk and laugh and play.
I love it so much; I wish I could stay.

THANKS for including me
as best as you can.
I appreciate you; you're part of the plan.

HOPE FLIES for me in a firefly;
It makes energy to shine
and with a cure so will I!

Printed in the United States
by Baker & Taylor Publisher Services